Growing Your Business

*Insights for startups and small business -
From a master entrepreneur*

New, expanded second edition

Dave Berkus

Published by David Berkus DBA The Berkus Press

For corrections, company/title updates, comments, or any other inquiries, please e-mail DBerkus@berkus.com

Second Printing, 2014
10 9 8 7 6 5 4 3 2

ISBN   978-1-105-04073-3

The content within this book has been previously published within the books, BERKONOMICS, and ADVANCED BERKONOMICS. Individual insights from this book are published periodically in Dave's emails and blog, www.berkonomics.com.

Groups may order copies of the book at a group discount by contacting Dave Berkus at 626-355-5375, or at dberkus@berkus.com .

Throughout this book, the Cambria type font was used for headlines, and text was set using the Calibri font.

The views expressed by the individuals in this book do not necessarily reflect the views shared by the companies they are employed by (or the companies mentioned in) this book. The employment status and affiliations of author with the companies referenced are subject to change.

Contents

INTRODUCTION

This book is the first in a series of eight short, easy to read books that guide an entrepreneur through the stages of creation, management, growth, and ultimately sale of a small business enterprise. And this is the second edition of this book, packed with half again as much materials the first edition, published in 2011.

Each section is an insight into another facet of starting a business that is not taught in business school or available in business texts, but rather the result of over fifty years of entrepreneurial experience with my own entrepreneurial companies and serving as investor, coach, mentor and board member for over forty entrepreneurial startups over the years.

Originally published as portions of three books, BASIC BERKONOMICS, BERKONOMCS, and ADVANCED BERKONOMICS, comments from entrepreneurs and professional managers after reading those books led to suggestions that I create separate mini-books for each stage of the business, to appeal to the interests of those at that stage of development, ready to absorb and implement insights that apply directly to the current stage of their business. Make them inexpensive and available as eBooks, they suggested, so that entire teams of managers could use the book as a planning tool and discussion prompt for the team in meetings.

And so this series of Small Business Success Books was born to address an opportunity. You can pick up this book and immediately relate to the insights, issues, opportunities, and exercises in this book right at the earliest stages of creating your business. This is not a replacement for "how to" books, courses, and consultants. It is a deeper opportunity to evaluate, plan, and execute strategies for growth based upon these insights that augment and amplify the usual "how to" materials available to entrepreneurs.

In this book, I'll tell personal stories from my fifty-plus years of entrepreneurial experience. But every one of us has a story to add to this mix, one of passionate entrepreneurism, sometimes inside an existing larger corporation, sometimes alone on a kitchen table, or back room desk. And it is a sure thing that many of us will have cogent, insightful additions to this caldron, culled from their own experiences. There's a place for these in the blog, www.berkonomics.com, and I welcome any and all for others to read and learn.

Dave Berkus

Arcadia, California

P.S. This is the sixteenth publication from *The Berkus Press*. I am very fortunate to have expert help this time from some very smart friends in the business, each of whom has volunteered to contribute one or more insights for this book, directly from their personal experience of working as an entrepreneur or with entrepreneurs. Here's a special thanks to these friends, whose contributions are definitely for your benefit. Whenever one of these excellent insights appear in this book, the first time each contributor's work appears, I'll insert a very short bio for that expert right below the headline. And as always, if no attribution appears for an insight, I'm its author - and to be blamed for any and all errors in judgment and accuracy.

Growing Your Business

There comes a time when businesses outgrow the original span of control of the entrepreneur. This critical period is a test of the entrepreneur's desire and ability to delegate, after successfully hiring the best of candidates to fill needed slots in the infrastructure. We hire the best people we can find, and turn from visionary entrepreneurs into (sometimes unwilling) managers of people. Most every entrepreneur experiences this as the company grows, even in its infancy.

There are risks inherent in growth. It is typical for companies to at least temporarily lose the focus upon quality that was such an integral part of the entrepreneur's vision when the company is in the midst of hiring and training new people, or when challenges to cash flow require scaling back. Often the first to go are those that test for quality or train staff.

In this short book, we'll examine two issues: achieving and maintaining a quality of product and / or service, and dealing with downturns in the business that can challenge the founder's focus upon the original vision for the business.

We start with setting expectations...

Fish in the giant ocean - not in a shallow creek.

This is like a Hans Christian Anderson parable, but aimed at you and your business... There are big fish and small fish, potential customers, all swimming in the sea that is your potential marketplace. You, the lonely fisherman, have to weave a net to catch your fish. Should your net be large and bulky, requiring more effort and expense to weave? Or should it be small and delicate, to catch those fish that would otherwise fall through the net?

The size of your market may well define the ultimate size of your dream. You can be the most successful coffee house owner in a city of ten thousand, or the founding CEO of the largest chain of coffee shops on the continent. Defining your market in a limiting way reduces the opportunity to exploit the larger potential that may be available to you.

If you attempt to create a manufacturing business where the total available market for your products is only $30 million, even success leading to a dominant share of the market would not allow your company to scale it to a size of great interest to investors.

This lesson is important. Companies grow proportional to the size of the market, and success cannot turn a limited market opportunity into a grand enterprise.

When we investors look at a business plan, we look immediately to see if there is research to support the claim of a large enough market to expect the candidate company to grow into the size projected. And we look to see if the size projected is large enough to interest us as investors, since that is directly proportional to the ultimate value of the company in a liquidity event.

To the point of the headline above, sometimes an entrepreneur claims that there is a large market, and attempts to make the case for growth into a grand scale company, sharing only a relatively small portion of that market. If the market claimed to be of a large size has no current, fast growing competitors, we must guess at the accuracy of the claim – something very unscientific. But if there are entrants already scaling, often we then can focus upon the differences and advantages our candidate entrepreneur brings to the market, a much more comfortable piece of work for the investors.

The size of your dream must be scaled to fit into the size of your marketplace. Be sure you can back up your claim with some form of research, then work to perfect the differentiation you offer against the competition.

And if your market truly is large but of unknown size, and if there are no competitors growing in the market, you must work doubly hard to convince investors of your dream. Yet, there are wonderful cases where entrepreneurs created and grew vast enterprises in new markets which could not be measured when their journey began. Think of FedEx, AOL, Microsoft, Cisco Systems, Facebook, YouTube, and tens of other billion dollar or larger players in markets that did not exist or were in their infancy when those entrepreneurs cast their nets.

Back to basics: Make your financials work for you.
By JJ Richa

J.J. Richa is a successful entrepreneur and technologist giving back to the entrepreneurial community in many ways, including his weekly Internet TV program on entrepreneurism, and participation in several mentoring programs.

How many units (widgets or hours) do you need to sell - and for what price - to be profitable? It's a simple question that sometimes takes us deeply into the murky waters of accounting detail. Yet, many companies have made huge mistakes when failing to properly calculate break-even for products and services. A break-even analysis is a very useful tool that can help you understand the sources of profit in your business.

A break-even analysis is a tool to determine the sales level at which the business is neither incurring a loss nor making a profit. In other words, the break-even point for a business is when the total expenses equal total revenue. To analyze break-even, you need to divide your income statement into three, not two sections, breaking out variable costs from fixed costs. So we will call it the *profit and loss management statement* instead.

In order to develop your profit and loss management statement, you need to do further analysis of your expenses, by accurately classifying them as either fixed costs or variable costs.

Fixed costs are those expenses that generally do not change in the short term regardless of how much you sell. Examples of fixed costs include general office expenses, rent, depreciation, most salaries, utilities, telephone, property tax, insurance and the like.

Variable costs are those expenses that change with the level of sales. These costs vary with sales because they are directly involved in making the sale. Examples of variable costs include direct materials, direct labor, cost of goods sold, sales commissions, freight, royalties, and the like.

Looking at your income statement, review the current classification of which expenses are fixed and which are variable. If a sale creates an associated expense, it's a variable cost. If a cost can go either way (fixed or variable), try to determine what portion of the cost is fixed and what portion of the cost is variable, otherwise consider it fixed. It may be helpful to ask yourself the following question: If the business did not sell any product or service, would it still have to pay a specific expense? If the answer is yes, that item is a fixed cost.

Most accounting systems will allow you to reclassify an account between fixed and variable expense and automatically move all transactions without disturbing the net profit.

Knowing your total sales, total variable costs and total fixed costs allows you to determine your *contribution margin* - basically the remainders after your variable costs are taken into consideration. Calculate your variable costs as a percentage of sales - and your contribution margin becomes the remaining percentage that would contribute to covering all other costs – the fixed costs. To obtain your break-even, you can divide the fixed costs by the contribution margin percentage.

If your fixed costs are not covered, there will be no profit. Losses will probably continue. You should fix what's broken in your business, provide for investment to cover expected losses until break-even, or halt operations to avoid draining all remaining resources. If your variable costs are not covered, you are in the wrong business, since you are selling your product or service for less than what it would cost you to produce such product or service.

One of the ways to be profitable is for you to know your break-even cost, sometimes call it your "nut," and set a goal for profits. Without having a goal, there is little chance for reaching your potential. Knowing the unit cost of a product or a service, you can determine how many units (widgets or hours) must be sold in order to reach break-even or a proposed profit level. This may be basic, but profit is the ultimate goal and measure of operating business success.

Execute the plan - or execute the planner.

It is all about execution. Waiting over a year to see results is too long, since your chance of mid-course correction is greatly reduced. To make the point, Harvard's Robert Kaplan believes that less than 10% of corporate strategies are effectively executed. Ouch!

If that is true, we are tolerant bunch. We carefully plan in long, dedicated sessions each year or so, then draw up a series of goals, strategies, tactics, objectives, targets, or whatever we want to name them. We hold all-company meetings where possible, and departmental meetings to roll out the new plan.

We set individual objectives and rewards to match these goals. Then we manage day-to-day routine execution, and periodically measure the results. Sound familiar? This is the description of a well-managed process within what should be a well-managed company.

And yet, Kaplan is close to right, whether it's 10% or 30%, it is a minority of strategies that are effectively executed. Why? Here is a list to use as a guide to better execution.

Make the plan simple to understand. Once deployed down one or more levels in the organization, like the old game of telephone, the corporate plan begins to look less like the original as each department attempts to adopt it and create departmental objectives to conform. A complex plan stacks the deck against all but those who created it at the top.

Put someone in charge of executing the plan. That may be you, but in some companies, that requires a dedicated individual tasked with removing roadblocks, measuring success, and reporting progress.

Provide feedback loops at each critical stage of execution. If the plan calls for increased revenues, measure output and efficiency as well as revenues. Look for leading, not lagging indicators of change.

Make sure you provide the resources necessary to hit the plan, including money, new hire authorizations, and above all, clear instruction and delegation form the top.

Listen to complaints, suggestions and warning signs. Respond, so that people know you are serious about execution of the plan. Modify what is not working. Then pivot, when necessary, to scrap part of the plan, and then rewrite it in order to meet its objectives.

If a plan has realistic goals and if you are reasonably able to provide the resources necessary to complete the plan successfully, you are way ahead of that other 90%.

But if you toss a plan out to others to execute, don't follow through until the end, fail to measure, or to provide needed resources, then you will deserve your fate. So take heed. If you go to the effort to plan, go to the effort to succeed.

Premature scaling kills businesses.

Venture capitalists sometimes make an error in directing their portfolio company CEOs to push resources to the limit and scale the business to immense size quickly, all to seize market share. The logic in this is simple: once a company has market share, other issues can be sorted out to monetize the market, make the company profitable, scoop up wavering competitors, or even sell the company to a larger firm looking for a large customer base.

This form of thinking has been unusually true during the rise of social media, where market share became the primary goal of a company, with revenues and profitability to follow later. It was true for Amazon and other visionary companies that grabbed market share during the early Internet era. But beware. Many, many companies accepting venture capital lost it all following this instruction. VCs have a goal of creating extraordinary value for their investors. Incremental profits from companies that later sell for three to five times their original value at the time of their investment may be considered great successes for founders but relative failures for VCs, who must hit for the fences with every early stage investment.

I've been involved as a board member of two such businesses, where venture investors came aboard and pushed management to immediately scale the business without regard for profitability, and without much regard for infrastructure. Both businesses scaled beyond what their market could absorb, and revenues did not build at nearly the rate of audience increase. The cost of each exercise was dramatic, far beyond what a founder-entrepreneur would order to be spent when using his or her capital or reinvesting cash flow from operations. Venture investors need large scale to make large exit valuations, or in many cases are not interested in maintaining marginal companies. To state it again, what might be a success to angel investors and to founders could be only of marginal interest to a typical VC.

Scaling a business is an art as well as a science. By definition, scaling requires the addition of fixed overhead, sometimes the kind you cannot shed easily, including leases for expanded space. Experienced CEOs often make it a habit to scale as a result of demand, reducing risk and mating cost to growth in revenues. Angel investors are more tolerant of this than VCs. Typically, when you bring a VC onboard, you increase the risk, the reward, and the definition of the size for a successful exit. Adding to this is the extra risk undertaken by premature scaling. It is important for you to realize that there is a fair tradeoff in valuation between a company with less outside investment and a lower endgame sales price, and one that shoots for a much higher valuation to justify a higher amount of outside investment.

Nail it; then scale it.

So your business has begun to take off. You've figured out your channels of distribution, pricing model and how to support your growing list of customers. Don't be alarmed by this next statement. *That's relatively easy.*

You can be the one to develop a product or service, promote it, and support it when you are a small operation. But what if you need to repeat the process of positioning, selling, and supporting your product ten thousand or more times as often as you do today?

It's worth repeating my *every three million dollar crisis* insight. You will have recurring crises as you grow your business. These are predictable and usually arrive in the same recurring order, and often with every $3 million in additional annual gross profit from revenues as you grow.

The first crisis is financial, funding the business, development, inventory, and marketing. The second crisis is organizational. At about the twenty employee level, the organization is too large for one person to handle internal operations, and a new level of management must be inserted between the founder and the existing team, causing communication and control issues that many founders have not experienced.

The third crisis is one of quality control. At about $6 million in revenue, there are so many new customers that product or service quality is stretched to the limit, and complaints about quality surface in quantities you never experienced previously.

Guess what? And, at about $9 million in annual revenue, the cycle repeats, with financial needs for additional working capital and money for growth churning to the top of the problem stack. And, as you grow, the same class of problems returns but with a larger scale and more urgent cry for attention - and more ruinous if not solved.

It is important - no it is urgent - that you solve these problems and know how to spot them coming in advance. To scale any company to a large size, you must know how to solve the problems of production, customer service, working capital needs and more in order to keep the company on the rails. The cost in lost efficiency, customer referrals, and corporate reputation is too high not to make this a priority for a growing business.

Many of the insights in this book and the BERKONOMICS series deal with the issues of scaling your business. As you feel more and more comfortable being able to scale each portion of the operation, you will be able to focus upon other areas of weakness, spreading the risk out and into a manageable range, rather than overwhelming you and your growing staff with their magnitude.

But wherever possible, it is best to nail down the processes and structure before and as you scale the business, not in emergency response to issues as they develop and grow to threaten the enterprise.

Drive your recurring revenues.
By David Steakley

David Steakley, a past President of the Houston Angel Network, is a reformed management consultant. He is an active angel investor, and he manages several angel funds in Texas.

I have a positive fetish for recurring revenue. When I hear a company pitch a business model which I believe has the potential to acquire a customer once, and keep the customer paying for a multi-year period without further marketing expense, my ears perk up. Typical examples are software as a service (SaaS) models, or any kind of content-driven subscription model.

There are so many things to love about a company with this kind of subscription model. Especially for a provider of a virtual good or service, costs of goods sold do not scale with sales, as they do in the real world. In the virtual world, a much higher percentage of incremental revenue falls straight to the bottom line. In most businesses, you can look at the revenues all you want, and you can draw pretty pictures extrapolating the curve of revenue growth, but, usually, the reality is, the company needs to go out and sell the annual revenue all over again every single year.

With the right recurring revenue model, top line growth can really shoot the lights out. Each year, the company can commence with a reasonably predictable big portion of last year's revenues already in the bag.

It requires special capabilities and expertise to really capitalize on a recurring revenue model, and a different way of measuring success for both executives and investors. Subscription businesses typically take longer to get to profitability, because costs of developing the product or service, and customer acquisition costs, are front-loaded, while revenue is back-loaded. By conventional measures of company performance, a recurring revenue company can appear to be struggling at first, but you have to know what measures are predictive for this kind of company.

The key calculation is the cost of customer acquisition, compared to the gross margin contribution of the customer. If an analysis of the gross margin on a new customer acquisition reveals that customer acquisition costs can be recouped in two years, you're doing well. If you get back customer acquisition costs in one year, you're doing *great*. This assumes reasonably low churn of 10% or less.

The crucial turning-point for a recurring revenue model with a potentially massive market is the moment when the acquisition model is sufficiently effective, refined, and repeatable, so you can blow it out and scale it up. If you've got a favorable payback period for customer acquisition, and you can repeatedly perform the acquisition model, then that is the moment to forget about profitability and spend like a crazy person by scaling up the sales machine.

When you go to sell the company, you'll get paid based on the slope of the recurring revenue curve (up and to the right), and even if a company sale is not in your plan, you'll be glad you sacrificed current profitability for the longer term, if you've picked the right moment to go big.

I've always thought Steve Case was the early genius of this kind of thinking. In the late 90s, you could have had a hard time picking up your mail without finding an AOL software connection CD in the mailbox. AOL spent about $300 million sending out those CDs, and at one point, half the world's production of CDs had the AOL logo on them. The lifetime value of an AOL subscriber was about $350. Average customer acquisition cost was about $35. That extreme in postal spamming took AOL from an IPO market value of $70 million to a merger value of $150 billion when AOL was combined with Time Warner. Wow.

Recurring revenue companies have been changing hands in the last few years at four to six times' annual recurring revenue. Steve Case's Time-Warner bonanza of perfect timing may not be repeated any time soon, but the appetite for these kinds of companies is more robust than ever.

My story: Fail locally, one customer at a time.
By Frank Peters

Frank Peters made his money writing software for Wall Street. Today he is best known as the host of the Frank Peters Show, delivered via the web each week to tens of thousands of entrepreneurs, angels and VCs worldwide. Frank speaks and networks at angel events around the world.

We've all heard the modern day mantra: *Fail Fast.* It's good advice; the theory being that entrepreneurs can discover the flaws in their business models sooner, make course corrections and move in a more favorable direction.

In my case as a young software entrepreneur, I had a different approach: *Fail Locally, one customer at a time.* Perhaps like many businesses, mine started out painfully slow; wage-wise, I think it was three years before I earned $30,000. For me I had few alternatives; working for someone else had proved to be a frustrating experience. I became an entrepreneur by default. I was fortunate that I could write software and doubly fortunate that my despair at working for 'the Man' - and feeling compelled to strike out on my own - coincided with the dawn of the personal computer era.

I've often looked back and said that you didn't have to be a genius at that time. You just had to be lucky, write reasonably good code and land in an industry with some legs, and of course, treat the customer well. Prior to bombing out of corporate life, I worked as a management consultant and at a very early age I was dealing with the presidents of very large companies. This would serve me very well as my product moved from individual clients to entire Wall Street firms licensing my code. But there was something else at work here.

I can't imagine encouraging an entrepreneur to follow in my path, but for me, operating alone with no board of advisors, no business plan and no outside capital, I was making it up as I went. I look back and describe the early days as 'selling software out of the trunk of my car'. I would write code all night then get in the car around noon each day to make my rounds. On the West Coast, where I started, the stock market closed at 1pm and that's when my customers wanted to see me.

I was fortunate that these individual customers were well healed; they had the money and were looking for an excuse to buy a computer. As I look back, I can remember so many times where I benefited from good luck. Who would've guessed that a day would come when a major Wall Street firm would make a strategic decision to open high profile offices across Southern California? How would they populate these new fancy offices? They would lure the best and the brightest away from their current employers with fat cash advances – enough for a new car, and a new computer. I was a beneficiary of this development. When one of my clients was recruited away from a user, and all his new officemates saw his computer, pretty soon I was invited into the new companies for all those 'me, too' sales.

Oh, how I tortured these early clients! Ours was a 2-man operation in those earliest of days; I knew nothing of quality assurance. It would not be unlikely at all that a major update to the software would break critical features that previously worked fine. Flaws like these could cripple my clients, causing them grief, lost productivity and worse, a loss of good will with their clients. Thankfully, these mini disasters occurred in small sizes. I could fix the bugs and hand-deliver the repairs before I infected more clients. In this way I learned a great deal. I would take the slings and arrows of my disappointed clients face to face. And I would learn customer service.

Years later, when news of my product spread to Wall Street and I had my first appointments in these corporate offices, I was well prepared. My earliest job experiences had placed me in similar hallowed places; I was not overwhelmed. At this point in the company's life, I had developed a mature product used by thousands of happy individual clients who were clamoring for the home office to build interfaces to minimize their manual data entry. But maybe best of all, as we arrived in Manhattan to move my officer to the source, I arrived with a good reputation and, as I like to say, I hadn't pissed off anybody on Wall Street.

From this point the company grew like wild fire. People liked the product and by buying a license for everyone in their firms, these Wall Street executives were rewarding their hard working sale force. It was hard to believe, but this was a new concept back in the days of 'green screens' that only offered market pricing data to the people who made all the money for the firm. We became as popular as the *hoola hoop*. We went from our largest-ever sale of 3 licenses at one time to a thousand. In ninety days we sold three major firms; and this would only be the beginning of our rapid growth. I look back today and muse, "No one ever asked us if we could deliver all that software." And oh, did we struggle as we learned all over again how to provide customer service to these large and demanding new clients.

Could an entrepreneur follow this same business model today? I suppose that's what limited releases are all about. But in our case, our test clients consumed us for our first nine years of existence – no one would advise a similar strategy today. We were lucky that we were able to learn so many painful lessons on a small and local scale. By the time a large opportunity came along, we were ready.

The five kinds of risk in building your business

If you could predict a crisis within your business before its occurrence, wouldn't you move to prevent or reduce its impact? Making such predictions is a skill that can be developed, and here's one method of doing so.

There are five basic kinds of internal risks than a business faces over time. Of course, there are external risks that cannot be controlled or predicted, but can be planned for as well – natural disasters, sudden political or economic events that rattle the entire economy, and more. That discussion is for a future time. Here are risks you can address.

First, there is *market risk*. Will the marketplace accept your product? Is there a market for your class of product at all? Market risk is constant and should be of greatest concern to any executive or entrepreneur. Mitigating market risk is not easy. Someone within your firm must be finely attuned to the changes in the market, including subtle signs from competitors. If you are big enough to have a dedicated product manager, that person is a good candidate for this ongoing task, as is a marketing manager, who should be attuned to the changes in the environment.

Second is *product risk*. Totally controllable within your organization, the quality and durability of your finished product should be at the top of someone's job description. Whether it is you or a quality control manager, someone must assure that the product or service you send out to the world will not fail to perform at least to the level of customer expectation, if not to delight those customers most likely to be critical.

Third is *finance risk*. Too often the person you call your chief financial officer is trained in accounting, which is primarily a process of looking backward over events in the past. A real CFO must be one to project and plan for the future as well, aware of the need for increased cash during times of growth or market disruption, and aware of the weekly challenges of shifting cash flow. The worst thing a fragile, entrepreneurial business can endure is to run out of cash. Not only is the enterprise threatened, but confidence is shaken among employees, suppliers, even customers. Competitors have a field day when hearing about cash problems at a company; and the rumors they pass on can reverberate for months or longer after the problem is solved.

Fourth is *competitive risk*, which consists of two separate risks. Do you have a significant barrier to entry to keep competitors from undermining your effort? And does a competitor have a better story and product to compete effectively against your offering? Someone within your firm must be finely attuned to the changes in the subtle signs from competitors. These include having a current knowledge of competitors' hiring practices, pricing strategy, and more.

Fifth is *execution risk,* which is squarely on management to perform, to take the company to and beyond profitability. It is your job to oversee the constant gathering of information, efforts to mitigate these risks, and even to hold senior level planning meetings around analyzing data and asking "what if…" questions that bring out the doomsday scenarios that could hobble your company. Once defined, the obvious next step is to role play responses to each challenge, or even to put in place preventative measures well in advance for each identified risk.

When one or several of these events hit you and your team, and they certainly will someday, you'll be better prepared to respond quickly and with a more appropriate, planned response. That will reduce the possibilities of suffering a catastrophe, and will more quickly calm the many stakeholders who have reason for concern, looking to you for assurances.

Why not plan a series of meetings with the appropriate members of your firm to discuss these challenges as you and they identify them, and prepare a plan for overcoming each? The time it takes may well be the difference between survival and doom; or it may be the plan that distances you from your competition if events do occur in your mutual future.

White-label it: Make it 'YOU' inside.
By David Steakley

David Steakley, *a past President of the Houston Angel Network, is a reformed management consultant. He is an active angel investor, and he manages several angel funds in Texas.*

Companies can strike it rich by finding an element of business operations which many companies need, but few have the capability or expertise to execute with excellence – and then aim to supply that element. Sometimes this is called a *white label* strategy, because your customers offer your product as their own product, writing in their brand name on the blank label in your underlying offering.

But, more often, this is just the virtualization of what we used to call outsourcing. On the web, not only does no one know much of who you are, but no one cares how you sourced your widgets.

Bazaarvoice, a company in Austin, Texas is a great example of this kind of operation. To be quite frank, the first two or three times someone told me what they do, I couldn't understand it. My preconceived notions of the possible range of business models simply didn't include this one.

Basically, the company created software for online forums. Really, that's a business? Yep: revenues of over $100 million per year with a market cap around $800 million. The company identified an element of operations which almost every online retailer already has, or needs, but very few do well on their own. Moreover, the company's offerings allow the retailer to change a thing which may be seen as mostly a pain - into an engine for increasing sales, for sharpening the retailer's value proposition, for catching and solving problems before they become real problems. In short, the underlying value of that company is the old-fashioned underlying value of outsourcing (if there was one): *the outsourcer not only does it for you, the outsourcer shows you how to do it right, and does it at lower cost.*

Now listen to one of Bazaarvoice's short pitches: "Our industry-leading social commerce solutions capture & amplify user-generated content, driving the highest social media ROI, for the world's largest brands." Forgive me, but I had no idea what that meant.

I heard another pitch recently, for a company which must have been unknowingly inspired by that other obscure pitch. This one wants to supply product comparison mechanisms for online merchants. You know, those bubble charts of products and features, by model? Do you want zoom in your camera? How much zoom? How many pixels? Thank god I had finally grasped Bazaarvoice; otherwise I probably would have sent these guys packing.

There's a lesson in this for business operators. Look around your operations, and identify areas of cost which, as far as you can tell, do little or nothing to enhance the profitability of your operations - but, you must have them. Can someone do it better than you, and at lower cost? Have an open mind. You're used to outsourcing payroll, bookkeeping, and logistics. Just for an exercise, see if you can identify someone to outsource absolutely everything in your business.

You have only so much management bandwidth. It can only make you more effective - if you're able to focus your attention on the things you're best at doing – your core competency.

Back to basics: Better manage your cash flow.
By JJ Richa

J.J. Richa is a successful entrepreneur and technologist giving back to the entrepreneurial community in many ways, including his weekly Internet TV program on entrepreneurism, and participation in several mentoring programs.

"Cash is King." You've heard this so many times it sounds trite. But in *trite* often is *truth*.

Without sufficient cash, even the most profitable business ceases to exist. Cash flow is not about profitability; it is about timing - timing of cash flowing in and out of the business. No matter how much you sell, if you don't collect the money, you're going to go out of business. As business owners, we often get so wrapped up in selling our products and services that we forget to take the time to ensure we're managing our cash flow and receiving the money for those sales.

It is simply insufficient to focus only upon total sales dollars. It is as important to focus on the cash collection of those sales. Reacting to cash flow problems instead of planning ahead means you are already in a bad position. It is imperative to take proactive measures to stay on top of your cash flow and improve the bottom line. Here are some tips:

1. **Know your business' balance sheet.** Many owners focus on the business' profit and loss statement alone. It's a potentially fatal mistake because healthy profits can mask an impending cash flow crisis. You need a structured balance sheet that includes all the influencing factors including debts, interest payments, inventory, with special attention to "current assets" and "current liabilities" – those due within one year.

2. **Cash Flow Statement and Cash Flow Projection.** Many business people don't know how cash flow works and its significance to keeping their operation afloat. There are several different cash flow reports available from your accounting system. A cash flow statement shows you how much cash is going into and out of your business. A cash flow projection is a forward looking report that estimates your future cash needs. Be aware of when you expect lean cash flow patches coming up and plan accordingly. Avoid funding major purchases from your business' working capital unless you are sure you have the cash to cover it. (In *BERKONOMICS* lingo, Dave states emphatically: "Never use short term cash to pay long term debt or buy new major assets.")

3. **Require upfront payment on projects.** The upfront payment may be a down payment, a percentage of the full project, a full payment for capital equipment, or any combination so that your customers fund the project, not you.

4. **Set your terms to be due in full upon completion.** Get your money as soon as you can and if you can avoid standard 30 day terms, it would be better yet. Certainly don't extend beyond 30 days after you've completed your work. Offer small discounts for early payment as an incentive.

5. **Negotiate terms with your vendors.** Take advantage of credit terms and prioritize payments according to the consequences involved in becoming overdue. Ideally you want to extend your payment for 30 days or more. This will give you the opportunity to complete the work, bill and receive payments from your customers prior to paying vendors. Wages, taxes and direct debits must be paid on-time. Key suppliers may be prepared to wait, just to keep your business. Don't pay early just to get a discounted price unless the discount is better than being without cash.

6. **Implement a collection process.** Follow through when your customers delay payments because they're using your cash. Be diligent about collecting from your customers. Stay in close touch with major debtors as payment deadlines approach. This requires continuous surveillance, and often is missed by small businesses with limited time and resources – a mistake.

7. **Set up a line of credit.** Obtaining a line of credit from your bank for an emergency reserve is a smart move, since lending rates are for the most part less than the late fees your vendors charge. And you know the old adage: the best time to get money is when you don't need it.

8. **Use available finance products.** Overdrafts, premium funding, lease facilities, even business credit cards and cash flow funding products can all be good tools to help ease the squeeze. *Factoring* or *asset based financing / lending* allows you to sell your receivables for cash now, in lieu of waiting for customers to pay. Associated fees may be high, so it is imperative to ensure that the benefits exceed the cost of waiting for customers' payments.

9. **Owner draws.** Each dollar you take from your company reduces the amount of cash flow you'll have available for the business to grow. Minimize owner's draws and try to depend on a fixed salary.

10. **Taxes and Penalties.** Avoid incurring unexpected taxes and statutory penalties. This may require help from your accountant or CFO to schedule due dates for all taxes on a calendar. You may want to eliminate all payroll tax risk by outsourcing your payroll to a vendor that "impresses" the taxes for you. An important side effect of good tax planning is to save yourself the money and the stress.

It is worth repeating: the best time to seek money is when you don't need it. No one wants to provide cash to a business that is experiencing cash flow problems. All cash is not created equal and you should consider timing, amount, usage, cost, control issues and consequences.

Create your budget from the top. Plan downward.

Many people believe that bottom up budgeting leads to waste and misdirection. The advocates of top-down budgeting are strong in their belief that if you give each person or department no guidance, they will budget to their wants or specific needs, not to those that support a corporate goal.

So, they argue: Give your people a top-down generated target. Have them fit their plans into the target. This way the corporate financial and strategic goals come from the top, as they should, and all departments fit into those strategies with their contribution and their overhead.

Over many years, in in many companies, I've overseen budgeting both ways, and agree with the advocates that it is often masked waste in the form of allowances for unknowns, extra padding for protection, and even higher budgeted expense numbers to make the managers look good at the end of year by under-spending, that are found deep within bottom-up budgets.

On the other hand, often departments cannot fit their required costs into the structure required to meet a profit goal for the corporation, or just as important, corporate revenue goals. In both instances, top down or bottom up, negotiations between department and corporate managers require compromise. The difference is that in a top down budget, the discussion almost always centers on compromises to meet the corporate goal, a much more important discussion than one centered around department goals.

Budgeting from the bottom up more often works in non-profit enterprises, where many departments are involved deeply into the detail of staffing and program delivery, and where the goal of the non-profit is service, not profit.   Either way, a budget is a necessary road map for a successful enterprise, and should never be ignored or worked upon after the year is already underway.

Whatever it is, try to deliver it via the cloud.
By David Steakley

Everyone knows that software-as-a-service has displaced the old style of delivering enterprise software. You may have assumed that this has transpired as a natural evolution of technological capabilities. Wrong. The key driver is to shorten the decision path.

With old-school enterprise software, closing a sale required you to get the customer's lawyers to sign off on the software license; getting the customer's IT personnel to bless your architecture and grudgingly deign to allow your software to enter the holy chambers of IT; getting the green shades to issue a check which would often contain six figures or more; persuading the IT gnomes to buy adequate disk space, CPU power, terminals, and network capacity to allow your software to operate; and many other relatively impossible hurdles. It is kind of amazing, in retrospect, that any enterprise software was ever purchased.

Software-as-a-service, often sold in a *freemium* model with the simple features available at no cost, allows the individual end user to decide on a whim to try out your solution, and IT never even has to know! "Contract? Well, there was some funny language I clicked on..."

There's a lesson in this for any company which intends to try to sell to huge corporations: design a sales model which requires the least possible action by the customer in order to close the sale, that involves the least number of corporate personnel, and requires the smallest possible amount of cash outlay at the outset. The closer you can be to allowing the actual end user of your product or service to decide on his or her own to buy your product or service, the better off you are.

If this type of approach simply doesn't work for what you're doing, then you have to grit your teeth and plan for success, to overcome the inherent obstacles of selling to corporations.

There's gold in repurposing intellectual property.

Several times a month, I'd have lunch with one of my CEOs, and each time we'd find ourselves digging into the intellectual property developed by the company over the years, just to refresh ourselves about what the intended use was back then, and whether new developments or technologies might make these older ideas and patents relevant again.

Since I have been involved at the board level with so many companies over the years, sometimes I can see connections that might be missed by a CEO with a singular focus. So I was surprised and excited when one of these verbal fishing expeditions during a lunch brought up a technology the company had patented back in 1995 and forgotten. The Internet was young, and the patented product allowed a visitor to dial into a computer (does anyone remember dial-up electronic bulletin boards?) and be redirected to a screen that would allow the user to identify himself, pay any fees required for use and agree to the terms of service.

From my more recent experience, I recognized that this describes exactly what every guest must do when attempting to gain access to the Internet in a hotel, or Starbucks, or any of thousands of public places. And I recalled that there was a patent war starting to take shape in this segment, centered about who was first to patent just this guest access.

It turns out that our patent was years ahead of those others, and was general enough to cover all forms of access to the Internet, not just dial up. The CEO began what continues as a licensing effort and lawsuits to protect the patent that could be worth more money in the end than the entire corporation was worth before the discovery.

Intellectual property is the principle asset of technology companies. The value of old patents cannot be easily estimated as new technologies reinvigorate those patents for new uses, such as the one we discovered during lunch. So: do you have hidden treasure in your vault?

Growth! I sat in my own safety net while weaving it.
By Berni Jubb

Berni Jubb was an Inc.500 entrepreneur, after years as a senior marketing manager of a large computer company. He regained his senses, and now runs a small resort and restaurant in Costa Rica.

My First Startup...

...never started, nor did my fifth or sixth. My desire to run something stirred inside me early in life, but the first real entrepreneurial adventure finally took hold after a lot of failed experiments. Each one had a steep learning curve. And all were missing a key ingredient or two. One thing, though, that never bothers an entrepreneur is fear of the unknown.

The good thing was that I had a certain ability to see ahead of the obvious horizon so I could often find resources we didn't have, and grasp those issues we knew we didn't know about. It is not today's idea that makes the business a success, it is tomorrow's. It is not today's screw up that really messes up your business but the one yesterday that you didn't know about.

I digress for a moment with a business lesson direct from the hand of our mentor at the time, Mister Berkus himself. I was asked to explain my issue at a CEO round table for one of Dave's membership groups. The date of the round table happened to coincide with the clearing up of the remains of a nasty event that caused my company to teeter on the edge of bankruptcy. Of course it wasn't just one event that was the cause, as you might guess. It was mismanagement that caused the event - rapid growth and the simultaneous realization by our big vendors that we had grown faster than our ability to pay.

The notorious *credit crunch*, as Wikipedia puts it succinctly "is often caused by a sustained period of careless and inappropriate lending which results in losses for lending institutions and investors in debt when the loans turn sour and the full extent of bad debts becomes known." Ouch!

We thought we had a friendly banker as a lifeboat. But the creditors and our bank somehow realized our "growth problem" all at about the same time, and when we went to use our bank line of credit, the bank told us we had *blown it* and the line was withheld. Our suppliers had been careless lenders - and we had been careless borrowers of their credit. The bank just sent us ... condolences. We missed all the signals. And we were one of the *twenty-five fastest growing companies* in the INC.500 list at that time. Double ouch!

In three weeks of fast restructuring of our credit, tamping down our growth, reworking our marketing plan, repairing our inventories, calming down our vendors, working with our bigger customers (i.e. fixing everything), we saved the company, and the bank pitched in to support our new plan. The post mortem occurred at Dave's round table a month later. I will always remember Dave's observation when I smugly concluded with "we know how to deal with this kind of thing now." He snarled across the table with a knowing smile . . . something like "It won't be this Pink Elephant that will sit on you again." These days I always have an eagle eye out for unknown Pink, Purple or Magenta Elephants waiting to trample on something I haven't thought of or experienced yet.

But how do you see these things before they hit you? What kinds of detectors are available to avoid these things?   You can't stop an entrepreneur from starting a new business or activity that is viewed as hopelessly stupid by detractors - and merely insane by close relatives. As an entrepreneur, you have a genetic problem. The bomb disposal guy in The Hurt Locker comes to mind.

Entrepreneurs often crash headlong into these nasty, often dangerous and sometimes exhilarating experiences. I posit that in fact entrepreneurs sometimes tempt fate to get off on the experience - tread close to the edge to keep the fire inside burning. They sometimes don't care; they are often reckless adventurers. Or as one of the richest guys in the world is quoted as saying, "A real entrepreneur is somebody who has no safety net underneath him."

The problem is that we weave that safety net even as we sit in it, making the job doubly difficult.

Double down!

This piece of wisdom came from Jeff Bezos, founder & CEO of Amazon, during a board meeting for one of the companies where he sits as board member. Jeff asked the question "Is there anything big or small, which is working better than you expected? Is there anywhere we could double down?"

Bezos' point was that we spend a lot of time focusing on what's not working in Board meetings (especially during difficult times) and not enough time focusing on what is surpassing expectations and how we can "double down" on those areas. Often times the key levers in businesses are found in little things that are really outperforming, whether by intention or not.

Although the scale of those businesses Jeff Bezos works with is probably much larger than those we deal with, his question is intriguing for multiple reasons.

We worry over projections and fix our budgets to match, and then we manage to the revenue and costs of the budget.   But what if we separate ourselves from that mindset long enough to search for and find sparks of success sometimes buried within our sales statistics.   A geographic territory or single product in a larger product line, or a service that was developed as an afterthought: do any show unusual signs of breaking out and becoming unanticipated successes?

Do we have the ability to change our thought process, alter our marketing focus, take resources from other areas if needed, and double down to back up potential winners in the making? Most of us would track the increased revenues, look at those in the light of total revenue progress, and monitor the actuals against the budget. A visionary like Jeff Bezos might pivot to make the rising star a centerpiece of our focus, quickly adding resources to support it, and seeing how far we could push it to make an unexpected success.

We all should have our antenna up looking for what's working, and where we should double down.   Surprise breakouts are rare and wonderful, to be supported immediately to the limits of our resources. That's the way small companies become big companies. It's the way surprising new products and services emerge from the pack and create new market leaders.

Greatly exceed early customer expectations.

First customers are critical. Greatly exceed expectations at all costs.

There is so much history behind this insight, and so many stories that illustrate this point. Your first customers for any product or service form your reference base, the important group of allies that your marketing and sales people rely upon when attempting to create buzz and make a mass market for a new product. If you've been involved in the launch stage of any product in the past, you should recognize the overwhelming feeling of panic when initial customers make first contact with complaints about quality, functionality, speed of service or other critical part of the new release.

The best advice I can give is to allocate all of your resources to supporting the roll-out of a new product, at least for a short period. Respond immediately to every question and complaint. Capture every compliment and ask if you can use it for marketing purposes. If the product or service is especially complex or expensive, send someone from sales or marketing or even R&D to the customer location at the moment of first use.

Of course most of us have limited resources for such overwhelming support of a new offering. So make the first release a limited one, sized so you can support it with existing resources, even if that means releasing it to only three carefully chosen customers at first.

And I am serious about the "...at all costs" admonition in this insight. If you must provide a free backup unit, personal on-site service for a month, your personal cell phone number for the customer CEO, or any number of unexpected offers of superior service and accountability to those first customers, do just that. Make your customer a partner in the process. Send flowers to the staff in the department using the product for the first time if appropriate. Call the customer CEO and thank him for helping launch a product so very important to your success.

The result of doing this right will be to blunt criticism, reinforce compliments and provide a solid user base to build upon. And the alternative is a lost opportunity to shine, perhaps a first wave of negative public reviews that post and report across the Internet, and a loss of reputation and goodwill that will take years to overcome.

I don't know about you, but I would much prefer to spend dollars reinforcing a great first customer's experience than fighting fires in the marketplace after seeing negative reviews. Make sure your entire staff buys into this mantra. "These first customers are critical. You are personally empowered to do everything possible to exceed their expectations."

Wasted time is money lost.

There is a relationship between time and money that is more complex than most managers think. Fixed overhead for salaries, rent, equipment leases and more make up the majority of the "burn rate" (monthly expenses) for most companies. Since this number is budgeted and pre-authorized, managers tend to focus upon other things such as sales, marketing and product development issues.

There is an art to efficient management of a process, whether that is the process of bringing a product to market from R&D to production or developing a new product's launch program. What most managers miss is that every month cut from the time it takes to perform such tasks cuts the cost by the value of a month's worth of fixed overhead or burn. Although young companies rarely measure profitability this repeatedly, more mature companies usually can bring from five to ten percent of revenues to the bottom line in the form of net profit. Ignoring cost of product for a moment to make a point, saving a month's fixed overhead by making processes more efficient, could easily double profits for the year.

That relationship between fixed overhead and production time is as critical as any other factor in success of a young company. Many of the start-ups my various angel funds have financed died a slow death, not because of poor concept but because of poor execution, wasting fixed overhead and draining the financial resources from the company coffers.

In the technology sector where I most often play, extended unplanned software development cycles account for the majority of these corporate failures. We often accept that development schedules for young companies are almost always too optimistic. But we investors often allow too little slack in our estimates as well. The great majority of young companies developing complex products such as semiconductor-based products, new software-based systems and technologies based upon new processes greatly underestimate the time needed to bring the product to marketable condition. So the CEO comes back "to the well", asking for more money from the investors to complete the project. It is not a strong bargaining position for the CEO to ask for money to complete a product promised for completion with the previous round of funding. And professional investors often penalize the company with lower-priced down rounds or expensive loans as a result.

I have one story that remains as vivid in my mind as when it happened several years ago. Helping the founder create a company and build a much-needed product in an industry I knew very well, I served as chairman for the newly formed company, and along with my several rounds of early investment, led rounds of other angel investors in what I knew as a successful opportunity to fill a need in an industry I understood.

The company grew to be well known in this limited niche and was operating at slightly above breakeven, when the Board and CEO decided to seek venture investment from what we hoped would be a first tier VC firm in Silicon Valley. And we were able to secure that investment along with a partner from that firm joining our board. It did not take long for the partner to become impatient with the relatively small size of the opportunity. Dreaming of a company many times the size, he led the board to approve a complete reversal of course, even stating that the company should ignore the existing market niche completely and redesign the product for the broad Fortune 500 corporate market. Every one of us on the board expressed our concern that the time to make these product changes and position for the new, broader market, would eat away all of the company's capital. Promising the full weight of his VC firm's resources, the board voted to make the change against the best judgment of those of us who knew the original market niche so well and thought that there was growth to spare in that niche alone.

So the company turned the ship, slowly it seemed, as R&D worked to develop an appropriate product using the base of the original design.

Time slipped; fixed overhead continued. And exactly as you'd expect, there came the time when the company ran out of money as it ignored its original market. Surprise. Since the company slipped in its R&D schedule, the partners of the VC firm voted to not add new money to the company for the project. Not long after, the company was sold in a "fire sale" amounting to slightly less than the debt on the books. All investors, including the VC firm, lost everything. Do you remember a previous insight, that "the last money in has the first say"? That is what happened within the dynamic of the board, and the result is that the board was completely at the mercy of the "last money" VC to save the company in the end. Yes, there were other issues such as a protracted patent rights fight that drained cash, but the largest problem, inefficient use of R&D time burning fixed overhead, led to the demise of the company. Lots of good jobs were lost and many investors including myself were left with the question. "Why did the company abandon a profitable market, even if it could not generate $100 million a year in revenues?"

We will revisit the relationship between time and money again in future insights.

Haste makes waste; but to lag is to sag.

Here we examine the relationship between time, quality and competitiveness. If you are getting the impression from these many insights that complex relationships cause simple problems, you are right.

We have heard the "haste makes waste" ditty since childhood. There is little need to reinforce the obvious. On a larger scale, there are epoch stories of giant companies eating massive losses in a recall of product, often based upon limited testing before release.

A marginal example was the Intel release of the Pentium Pro and new Pentium II processor to rave reviews – until a math professor found an obscure error in the chip's code that made a rare floating point calculation error. Posting that finding on the Internet, quickly Intel found itself defending against fears by others using the processor for math work that the processor could not be relied upon. Intel rushed to fix the bug and offered to replace the processor to anyone requesting such a replacement. At a cost of millions and a reputational hit, Intel recovered. The lesson here is a bit obscure, since it is not clear whether the kind of testing then common in processor design would have surfaced the error. It is quite clear that such an error would be found immediately today based upon changes in testing procedures made by all processor manufacturers after that event.

The waste from haste in this example was in not pre-thinking of enough testing scenarios for a new product. There is always a trade-off between cost for testing, time to market and risk of problems.

Perhaps better examples to point to are easy to find in the toy industry, where recalls because of small parts that could be swallowed by infants or lead-based paint or flammable components make the news on a regular basis.

And the other side of this coin, "To lag is to sag", addresses the two issues of loss to the competition because of delays in release of a new product, and burning of fixed overhead while products are redesigned.

It becomes obvious then that there must be a balance somewhere between rushed release and too much rigor in pre-release planning and testing. Perhaps that balance can be measured in estimating what a company could endure in lost overhead and hits to reputation before becoming crippled and unable to recover. With that measure based upon pure estimates, the balance point changes between companies, with the largest, most profitable companies able to suffer the most risk as to resources, and the smallest suffering by far the most when measuring reputation.

No second chance to create first quality.

Let me illustrate this insight with a personal story. As my enterprise computer software company which produced innovative lodging systems for hotels and resorts grew quickly, we found ourselves straining to keep up with the hiring and training of good customer support representatives, a critical part of the equation then and still so today in the 24 hour environment of hotel front desk operations. If a front desk clerk called support at 11.00 PM in the evening, it usually meant that there were guests lined up waiting to check in, anxious to pass beyond this necessary but inconvenient bottleneck between a tiring plane ride and a comfortable bed. The result would be very frustrated clerks facing angry guests if the wait was too long. It was simply not acceptable to be backed up in customer service, forcing either a ten minute wait or a call back from support.

It took several months to hire and train enough new support reps to keep up with the rapid growth of our company. But the problem was solved, and response times returned to "immediate" for at least this class of customer call. There was no wait, and the quality of response was rated as "excellent" by callers later surveyed. But "There's the rub" (the snag) wrote Shakespeare in *Hamlet.* It took two long years for the company to fully recover its lost reputation after the actual problem was fixed to the satisfaction of all.   Aided by salespeople from competitors and long memories from unhappy customers, the myth of continued quality problems in customer support bounced around the industry for those years, until finally good press, great experiences and a marketing campaign together overwhelmed bad memories to put this issue to bed.

If the problems had been in product stability and customer service together at the same moment, there might not have been enough time and resources to recover. There are plenty of young companies that died trying to recover from such a combination.

Your reputation hinges upon delivering a quality product at the moment of release, and maintaining product quality throughout its life. The smaller the company, the more is at stake. There are fewer resources and much less of a reserve of good will among the customer base to absorb a problem release or in the example above, inability to fill the void in customer service created by rapid growth.

Demand pull – cost push.

Place your cash bets behind proven demand.

The term, "demand pull – cost push" was created by the great economist, John Maynard Keynes, to describe the two primary drivers of economic inflation. Demand pull: too much demand for a product or service and not enough supply cause a competition for the product that drives prices higher without increasing the intrinsic value of the product. Cost push: labor or parts costs increase, causing the product or service to be priced higher without adding intrinsic value. As a student of economics, I studied Keynes and his many theories of macro and micro economics, but this one kept returning to me as an excellent way to describe a completely different business principle.

All of our enterprises have limited resources, even the largest of the Fortune 500, and especially the smallest of competitors in a market. Most new product introductions are planned with a broad campaign aimed toward the whole of the marketplace, committing resources such as money and manpower to the effort. I have learned over the years that this may not be prudent. Instead, seeding various segments of the market, vertical niches, with focused attention in form of marketing and sales efforts, will quickly yield positive results from some niches and perhaps no interest from others. It is upon the moment of understanding which niches respond positively to the new offering that a company should push costs into increased marketing and sales efforts into those niches, concentrating fire power and overwhelming the niche, instead of making few waves in an ocean of broad opportunities and becoming lost in the process. To describe this, Keynes comes to mind. Push the costs into market niches where you seed your marketing, and experience the pull of customer demand as a result. *Cost push – demand pull.*

Hire ahead of need only when growth is stable.

Many companies have made the mistake of using the forecast to plan and executive hiring of new employees so that they could be trained and up to speed when the demand arrives. Although such a practice does add to overhead by bringing employees aboard before they become economic contributors to the bottom line, there is much to be said about service quality by having trained employees on the front line when the customers want and need them.

There are periods in any economy or industry segment when growth seems steady and there are few warning flags ahead. In such instances, it is much less risky for a company to execute its plans for spending in coordination with forecast revenues. But there are many more times in which the near term future is far less predictable, and when early hiring decisions may be just the wrong move, reducing flexibility and reserve resources. It is during such more common times, that you should consider using temporary employees to fill demand as needed, even if brought aboard a bit early for pre-training. And increasingly, there are off shore service providers able to contribute to production and service, expanding and contracting at will, with some sacrifice in control and sometimes in quality.

Further, a company suffers in its reputation with its employees when hiring and firing in short cycles to meet short term needs, unless those brought aboard are hired as temporary or seasonal workers. Every employee wants a stable work environment and does his or her best work in a culture of mutual trust as to continued service as a reward for good work. Constant interruptions in the chain of command, changes within the ranks and threats of impending layoffs together combine to form one of the greatest impediments to efficiency and a strong corporate culture.

Growth calls for more cash, not less.

Here we must do a little math calculation together to make a point. Assume that your gross margin from sales is 50% for ease in calculation. Assume 30 days to collect receivables from completed work, and 30 days to complete the work. Finally, assume a fixed overhead equal to all of the remaining 50% of revenues, just for the sake of making this point. Zero profit. Now consider an increase in your revenues from $1 million a month to $1.5 million, the extra $500 thousand to be billed in 30 days upon completion of work. During the first 30 days, you pay out over that period $750 thousand, the fixed overhead and cost of sales. That's $250 thousand more than last month, putting you in the hole. You bill the $1.5 million on the 30th day and start the clock, waiting 30 days for receipt of the cash. During that time you receive the $1 million you billed the month before but pay out another $750 thousand in overhead for the following month. Where do you sit at the moment before collecting the $1.5 million billed last month? You are down an extra $500 thousand beyond the breakeven amount when you were billing a steady $1 million a month and paying out 50% for cost of sales and 50% for pre-ramp overhead. It took your company finding or funding $250 thousand a month for two months to finance an increase of $500 thousand in revenues. Surprise? Most managers are. If the growth continues, the amounts needed just increase and increase, until fixed overhead is no longer such a large part of revenues (growing more slowly than revenues), and perhaps margins increase with buying power and efficiencies of mass production.

With an asset-based bank line and a limit far higher than current need, a company can borrow against those receivables and eliminate at least the second $250 thousand of cash needs, since the receivable "pledged" for the bank line increases by $500 thousand. Most companies have little headroom in their asset-based bank lines, and such expansion of revenues can be accommodated only for a while before the line is borrowed to its maximum.

Growth requires its own unique form of working capital cash planning. The mere fact of rapid growth is not enough to create capital within most organizations until the growth becomes more stable and receivables collections catch up with costs advanced to the various resources to "buy" that growth.

Contribute to A-M-D, or support someone who does.

- **A.** *Accumulate or acquire (product line, breadth of services)*

- **M.** *Marketing or merchandising (expert and diligent use of resources)*

- **D.** *Distribution (adding channels and reinforcing relationships)*

Let me credit CEO Erik Hovanec for this one, whether he originated it or recast it from his past. As his chairman, I have watched him masterfully focus his employees all toward a common theme aligned with the company's goals. The genius of this insight is that no employee is exempt, even those in accounting or human resources. Everyone supports the contribution to AMD in some way, or, according to Erik's challenge, should not be here breathing the air, taking valuable space and consuming scarce resources.

People in R&D, business development, purchasing or production all fit in to the "A" of the equation. Without constantly improving or increasing products to offer, a company today is quickly overtaken by its competition. Stagnant companies usually can trace their inability to gain market share upon the "A" area first, and management should pay particular attention to putting resources into this important focus of the company.

Without the "M", effective marketing and or merchandising, sales people and distribution channels quickly dry of leads and must fight for attention beside better branded competitors. Marketing is the area least understood, often least funded, and perhaps one of the most important within any company. Even with the best products or service, companies fail for the want of good marketing.

For many industries including those with Internet-based sales entities, you cannot have enough channels of distribution, the "D" in this insight. Some management will argue that channel conflict is one of the worst ways to lose the loyalty of distributor and direct sales resources. I'd counter that a cohesive distribution strategy calls for a coordination between inside and outside distribution resources by management, not a competition for customers using inside resources to compete with outside distribution. There are many ways to allocate or split a product or service in the marketplace: by size of customer, geographic location, market segment, or even agreed-upon rules to protect open competition between the distribution groups.

Sometimes, a company must create a unique brand to self-distribute in competition with other distribution resources. Many manufacturers have successfully created "OEM" labels for branded retailers wanting to distribute under the retailer brand, without disturbing other distribution channels. And many wholesalers have successfully created a new self-managed retail brand for direct distribution in competition with current retail distribution channels.

Focusing your entire staff on a simple, understandable set of functions in support of the goal is a masterful way to increase productivity, create urgency and measure contribution of individuals to the common good. Remember: A-M-D.

Celebrate each victory!

Growing companies give rise to many events that great managers will take advantage of to create and shape the culture of the company itself. Each new plateau in revenue growth, each time a month's orders hit a record, each large order from the sales department, all of these and more give rise to opportunities to celebrate publicly. Everyone in a stressful corporate environment loves to pause and relish the latest victory.

Each time our company would hit a new milestone, I would make a public announcement personally, then, with my payroll person in tow, walk the floors of the various company buildings handing out $50 or $100 bills to all employees as instant bonuses. You wouldn't believe how much people seemed to enjoy the boss' visits. The goodwill created and buzz that continued for days were well worth the small cost. Everyone got the message: growth is great, and everyone is treated equally in celebrating. Each distant or foreign office was included, although not often enough with personal delivery services. This is different from "managing by walking around", which requires no reason or structure other than the willingness to listen and learn from people on the line.

Many companies have a bell hung somewhere in or near the sales bull pen, rung each time a sale is consummated. Managers should encourage everyone within the hearing of the bell to stop long enough to applaud, reinforcing the unanimity of approval for each new sale.

Victories that shape a company's culture can take many forms. Years ago, an emergency phone call was directed to my office from our distributor in Australia. Their largest customer, Hamilton Island Resort, had just suffered a fire that destroyed the building containing their large minicomputer installation. No-one was injured, and there was a backup from the night before stored in a safe location. But there was no replacement machine in Australia, and each day that guests checked out without paying their bills amounted to a day where cash flow was at least temporarily reduced by at least $250,000, not a small amount as it accumulated. Simultaneously, we had a new machine with identical specs on the shipping dock for a Florida installation at a property whose managers were pushing the company for an instant delivery. I made the decision without pause to redirect the shipment to Australia that day. Then I immediately called the CEO of the Florida customer to explain. Not too happily, he acquiesced. Everyone within the company knew of the problem and of our instant reaction to aid our customer, even in the light of pressure from the Florida customer now back in line for shipment. We oversaw the successful installation in Australia the next day in a temporary building and our people helped key in data subsequent to the backup. Everyone knew from management's actions and their own efforts that the customer comes first, always. This story has a second happy ending. We engineered a rerouting of the Florida order a week later so that the computer to be shipped would be the 1,000th of its model. Before packing it in its large shipping crate, we held a party in the shipping dock for all employees, with streamers and cake and the world's largest greeting card – hundreds of sheets of continuous form computer paper, which every employee from software programmer to shipping clerk signed with a message of thanks and goodwill for the Florida customer's sacrifice. That week, we scored two great customer stories and more goodwill throughout the organization.

Victories come in many shapes, sometimes when least expected. Celebrate them all.

You are your company's moral compass.

Years ago, when I was CEO of my record manufacturing company in Hollywood, I happened to walk around the plant into the press room just as Bobby, one of the employees' favorite coworkers, was offering stolen merchandise to his fellow pressmen from a bag he was carrying. He halted, and waited for me to react, obviously caught in the act. Everyone loved Bobby, a hard worker and good friend. But I fired him on the spot; the only possible response to the situation presented me so suddenly. After initial shock, a number of employees came to me that day and said that they understood how hard that decision was, but that they knew it was the right thing to do.

You will find many times during your management years when such decisions are placed before you, requiring quick unwavering response to an ethical challenge to you or your company. How you comport yourself in these situations is absolutely the litmus test for how your company culture will reflect your actions. Take home company supplies for personal use? Your employees will surely follow your lead, no matter what the policy. Treat personal expenses at company cost, and your sales people will feel just fine doing the same until caught. Behave without regard for an individual's dignity when separating an employee who is a direct report, and other managers will feel little compunction to spend the extra time and energy softening their actions. Alter any accounting result for the sake of making a month look good, and your accounting department will get the message that GAAP accounting is just for show.

It is not easy to always be the moral compass for the organization, but it is the right thing and cannot be compromised. And you will continue to enjoy the stories of times taking the high road as retold to you by your employees over time.

Help your associates advance their careers.

We'd all like to retain our best managers and employees forever or at least for as long as possible. But sometimes our corporate wants and needs conflict with what is best for an employee and his or her career development. We cannot legally stand in the way of an employee resigning to pursue a dream, but we can leave a bad taste with that person and chip away at our corporate culture by not cooperating or even helping the employee move on. It doesn't take much to publicly wish a departing employee well, to throw a small celebration, to coach the outgoing person if asked, and to listen and receive fair criticism at the moment of the exit interview. And sometimes, the story that results is one that joins the ranks of super-tales, to be told again and again. Here is one such departure story I tell often.

Tom rose through the programming ranks to become the chief architect of my software company, with 26 programmers in his fold. The company had grown to 233 employees and served 16% of all automated hotels worldwide at that time. Each week, Tom and I would have an informal lunch and discuss issues that ranged far and wide. Tom almost always had ideas to contribute, particularly about marketing programs and opportunities.

One day Tom came to me and said, "I want to transfer to marketing. I am tired of programming." "But Tom", I protested," you are in charge of the family treasure. All of us depend upon you. Oh, the humanity…" Tom insisted, and nothing I could say would stop him from resigning, selling his home, and moving away. Five years later, I received an email from Tom. I keep that email in my leather note portfolio, carrying it with me wherever I go, pulling it out often to read portions to audiences during my workshops, or just for fun to fellow private equity investor friends. "Hello again, Dave," it began. "After looking around a lot, I have landed as employee number seven at a Seattle-based startup called Amazon.com." Tom goes on to extol the opportunities, describe his job in marketing with creative opportunities at every turn, and then… "My founder is in round two of capital-seeking, looking for increments of $100 thousand, and if you'd like, I'd be happy to introduce you..."

In one of the most understated several word paragraphs in history, I responded by email, "Gee, Tom. Good to hear from you. Keep me informed." After recounting this story, I then ask my audience to guess what an August, 1995 angel stage investment in Amazon might have been worth at the IPO, getting lots of range in the responses. The answer is $31 million. $31 million return from $100 thousand investment, or 310 to1. That story always gets a laugh as most everyone of us recalls the deal we didn't do, the investment we didn't make, the opportunity we shunned that turned to gold.

So you never know what good things will someday come, especially from talented, driven associates you nurtured but released into the wild when their time had come.

Plan for your R&D Tax.

There is a life cycle for any product, and it is much shorter on average today than five years ago, especially in the technology world.

Companies that are successful with their first product must begin thinking about the costs of additional products or of that product's replacement well before any evidence of a peak in sales is noticed.

There are rules of thumb for various industries in creating a reserve for research and development. To attempt to find an average number, companies should "tax" themselves by reserving some percentage - say ten percent of their net revenues - for research and new product development.

It is a certainty that even with patent protection, a successful product will be challenged, duplicated, even exceeded by competitors, and within increasingly shortened time periods. It is a difficult concept, but a necessity of the modern age, to plan to obsolete your own successful products before someone else does that for you.

Better is the Enemy of Good Enough.

Getting any product to market is an act composed of a series of compromises in quality, product perfection, feature-functionality, and cost effectiveness. If every development engineer could control the release date of the component or product for which s/he is responsible, the dates for completion would certainly extend outward and vary from plan.

When there are multiple parallel developments of components to fit into the whole product, the slowest component determines the speed of completion for the final product. One designer, one engineer, one developer seeking to achieve a degree of perfection to meet a personal level of satisfaction is capable of derailing an entire complex project.

And yet, who would not want the highest quality product to place into a competitive marketplace? Who would not want a "better" component or product? By its very nature, "good enough" defines the acceptable market level of quality, price, feature-functionality, and salability. That standard certainly varies by any requirements for product safety which surmount all others. That one standard aside, all of us must internalize the short mantra that is the subject of this insight: *Better is the enemy of 'good enough.'*

Keep constant contact with key customers.

An executive's job is not easy, nor is there much time in a typical day for outreach of any kind. Especially in a growing company, the CEO is drawn into daily process issues by all of his or her direct reports, often responding to questions and problems, leaving little time for strategic thought.

And that behavior results in leaving little time for outreach to the most critical possible component in your chain – your key customers. During CEO roundtables which I attend regularly, fellow CEO's analyze a compatriot's use of time during the once-a-year personal presentations each makes in turn. If the presenting CEO is honest in the analysis of actual time spent each week, it is often revealing to all to see how many hours are spent turning inward toward meetings, operational management, or responding to emails or texts sent by others.

As a group, we set a bar of fifteen percent as the minimum amount of time each week that a good CEO should spend reaching out to the company's key customers in a proactive attempt to find issues, trends, unmet product needs, and of course create bonds that make their jumping to a competitor more difficult.

Do customers know what they want from their suppliers for future products? We often ask our sales people to "find the pain" and show how our product solves that pain problem. But it was Henry Ford who famously said, "If I'd asked my customers what they wanted, they would have said 'a faster horse'."   Some new products arrive with no frame of reference. FedEx, the automobile, the Internet, and many more examples, prove that there can be a significant market for ground-breaking ideas.

Do customers know what they like when they see it? Of course they do. So why not show a prototype, asking for input to improve it or adapt it to the needs of the customer?   With that kind of interaction, the customer becomes a partner in development, tied to the success of its outcome and much more willing to purchase it when completed.

Is business built upon good relationships? Of course it is. And who is best to create closer relationships at the top than two CEO's speaking personally without distraction?   I have won deals after forming such trusting relationships, and have lost deals to those who have beaten me to the opportunity.

The challenge is also the opportunity. A good CEO spends time with critical customers and values the feedback and relationships that result.

Remember the GOAL!

Often we joke together as CEOs that our goal is "world domination" or "to crush the competition." But no matter how stated, the primary goal of an enterprise is to make money.

How do you measure progress toward such an undefined goal? We measure it by profit or revenue in dollars. But that is a number in a vacuum without at least two other measures: return on investment (ROI) and percentage of net profit to revenue.

Microsoft generates billions of revenues and profits and even has a high ROI and high net profit percentage. But some of our small businesses have even higher percentages of return on investment and percentage of net to gross. So the amount of money made is a number in a vacuum without the rest of the tools to tell the story.

The next time someone tells you that their goal is world domination, you might politely smile and remind them that a more modest goal might better serve the stakeholders over time and that it might be a bit easier to accomplish.

Find and build recurring revenues.

Most every business can take advantage of continuing, recurring revenues from its customer base. Sometimes, products are designed to make all of their profit upon the recurring revenues from supplies or support. We immediately recall the razor and blade analogy to illustrate the point when planning product development and release.

Xerox in its formative years, even though barely having enough cash to market its then revolutionary copier, elected to lease rather than sell the units. Even though that reduced short term earnings, lease revenues over time far outweighed any combination of sale and maintenance revenues, and Xerox grew into a major company based upon its innovation and its recurring revenues.

In examining mature software companies in vertical markets, one of my first questions is to ask for the percentage of total revenues coming from recurring sources – leased software, maintenance agreements, or monthly retainers. Usually that amount exceeds 50% of total revenues, and is often much more. Mature businesses bring less in an M&A transaction than fast-growing companies, but the stability of recurring revenues always gives comfort to the buyer and allows the seller to slow the sales process, find multiple candidate buyers, and create increased demand for the company.

Think of the portion of fixed overhead covered by recurring revenues. If the gross profit margin averages fifty percent in a service company, and if fifty percent of all revenues come from recurring sources, then it is probable that the company is stable and operating at or above breakeven.

And in a sale of the company, it is usually better for the seller who will command a bonus valuation based upon some multiple of recurring revenues due to the comfort value to the buyer and the increased lifetime value of each customer to the enterprise.

Never handle a paper twice.

We are not dealing with personal time management with this series of insights, except when it helps immensely to make a better manager of you and me. All of us have time management tips and tricks to help us get through the day. I have a mantra I try to live by, and it has helped me more than you know over the years. "Never handle a paper twice" may be extended to include reading and acting upon emails, messages, and any written distraction. It is human nature to filter through the stack or inbox, looking for the important items. And that certainly has defensible merits. But to find what is important, we usually have to at least scan a document or email, engaged for no less than a short moment and perhaps for the full reading of the document before moving on to look for important issues to resolve.

But there is good research to back up the statement that returning to a reading from a distraction causes the reader to lose up to 20% of his or her time in getting back to speed in mentally processing the document and its issues. By trying my best to adhere to the "never twice" rule, I quickly delete most copy-all emails not addressed to me, and all junk, but handle each personally addressed email as it opens in the reading pane. The exception is an email with an attachment that appears long and involved, such as an executive summary of a business plan. Those get shuffled into a separate inbox for later review, without exception. Using this policy, I get through my several hundred non-spam emails each day faster than I used to, and with more focus upon those with response required than if reading and returning to the issue at a later time, especially if not in the same sitting. Exempt emails from your superior and those marked as urgent, both of which should be either directed to a special handling inbox or culled out from the rest immediately.

Wouldn't you like to regain some percentage of your time with little or no effort? Try this one.

Sift your time through the filter of your vision.

All of us are pressed for time, always attempting to balance the overwhelming demands of business with the basic wants and needs of family. In earlier insights, we have examined the need for and care of your corporate vision, and how to develop and nurture that vision through to creation of a corporate culture, goals, strategies and tactics. Now we get personal.

Each of us makes many decisions each day as to where to spend the days' time. Many of our decisions seem to be made by others, with meetings scheduled requiring our attendance, the landslide of emails arriving hourly, emergencies popping up requiring immediate attention, and more.

The first thing to do as a senior executive is delegate whatever comes across your desk that is not directly relevant to your enterprise's and your own strategic importance to the company. That means teaching others how to do some of the work you have been doing, sometimes loading more upon another's full plate. We must assume first that your delegation effort is to those lower in the food chain. (They in turn must learn to delegate using the same filter, or if there is no next level, shed those items not in their strategic path.) Second, you have a vision for the company which you ask everyone to buy into as they plan and execute during their year. You should remember to take your own advice, and filter your activities through the needs of your vision, again shedding even more insignificant activities that cross your desk.

Who knows? These two filters when put in place might just give you back enough time to add a few enjoyable processes to your day, just for the lift they give. We can dream, can't we?

You are watched, mostly when decisions are tough.

If you have been in management or an entrepreneur long enough, you will have experienced the gray area of decision-making where ethics, the law, your needs and expediency all collide. This is the time when you are paid the big bucks, and when others aware of your plight will be watching most carefully. It is also the time when you demonstrate your true courage to your contemporaries.

I have a Ph.D. friend who teaches a graduate course in entrepreneurism at a local university. He uses the case method to place as many of these types of decisions in front of his students as possible each semester. And the responses from students are predictable. When faced with a gray area decision, the first response is to follow the letter of the law, the rules, the 'right thing to do.' The professor then injects one or more new facts into the case, and the students waiver, more and more as the new facts are analyzed, reducing their fervent enthusiasm for the "always right thing" stand. By the end of each case, most everyone has a position that has modified since the first impression. Then the professor reveals the action the company executive took to resolve the problem, often one not considered by the students.

Consider the case of the company with goods on the dock ready for shipment, a company with an accounts receivable-based asset credit line that is already at its limit due to the calculation by the bank of availability based upon current receivables. The rules for "pledging an invoice" as collateral for borrowing call for attaching signed shipping documents showing that the goods have been picked up by the carrier, at which point the title transfers to the customer and the invoice from the company is "good". The senior manager, whether the CEO or CFO or head of shipping, walks over to the location where the shipment sits waiting for pickup, complete with paperwork waiting signature by the carrier driver. The manager picks up the paperwork, and using a blank page inserted into the stack, signs in place of the carrier driver. He then pulls out the now signed company copy and returns to his office with just that copy in hand.

Within an hour, the bank receives a copy of the invoice with the signed shipping document attached, along with a very standard request to borrow the 80% of the invoice amount. The bank clerk approves, adds the amount to the loan and company's cash account, and all is well. Or is it?

Invariably the students correctly point out that the company manager falsified a document, which surely is against the law since an invoice was pledged to the bank that was not represented by a completed shipment. After this discussion, the professor adds that he forgot to tell the students that the shipment made it to the dock minutes after the day's carrier pick-up and that payroll is due tomorrow and the cash must be in the bank today to cover the direct deposits. The only way to get that cash today is through the credit line borrowing, and after all, the carrier will pick up the completed shipment tomorrow morning. Now the students debate ethics against legality against pragmatism. Some hold their positions. A missed day of payroll is a small price to pay for even this small breaking of the law. Others state that the reputation of the company as a reliable employer is at stake, and that the employee loyalty will be shaken if payroll is delayed for even one day. The students divide somewhat evenly over the minor infraction.

Then the professor reveals that the shipment on the dock is only a small partial shipment but that the invoice that was pledged to the bank was for the entire amount of the order. Now the students debate whether the manager should be fired or the bank informed of the obvious falsification. And the professor adds that the manager in this case is the CEO himself.

Interesting enough, no student has yet suggested the Kobayashi Maru solution (*remember, Star Trek?*) where the CEO merely thinks outside the box or changes the rules. The CEO could have immediately called the carrier and offered a significant sum, say $500 for a quick custom pick up of the partial order, or called for the current location of the driver and found a way to load the shipment into a car or truck to meet the driver, or even plan to drive to the carrier's dock itself.

You get the idea. Decisions go from black-and-white to gray to black-and-white again, based upon relative knowledge of the facts and of course, the law. Just as a personal test, what would you do if you were the manager? Or if you were the shipping clerk observing this happening regularly? Or if you were the bank auditor discovering that this was a regular practice?

A CEO or manager's life is not simple. But there are lines, both ethical and legal, that just cannot be stepped over, difficult as the result may be. Each of us is tested in subtle and sometimes very public ways often during our careers. It is a simplification to state that the "good guys finish first", but looking back over long years of experience, there is a great deal of long term truth in that statement.

Get to your goal by the most direct route.

There is more money lost in businesses today from inefficient processes than any other single area. Yet this is not a place where most managers feel comfortable deconstructing and rebuilding. Somewhere out there is a consultant or future employee (or even suggestions from present employees) that will provide the roadmap toward making your processes run more smoothly, more quickly and more inexpensively. As a byproduct, process quality is likely to improve as well.

No matter what your company produces, there is surely a more efficient way to approach the process. Start by carefully restating the goal for the process, such as "produce 500 quality units per day" and create metrics to measure the present output and quality (rejects or time lost) with this goal. Look inward, forming a "tiger team" from within your organization to define the steps presently taken to reach the goal, and make improvements in increments that can be put into effect and tested quickly. The best reward for those involved in improving a process is to receive the kudos from management and themselves for making dramatic improvements in their internal processes.

If internal resources cannot handle the solution, it is time to find an outside resource that can. Either way, someone must start with creating a map of steps from start to completion, breaking it down to measurable sized increments. Look first at whether some steps are creating a bottleneck or quality breakdown affecting subsequent steps (see insight 81 following this). If improving individual steps are not the solution, then scrap the process entirely and attempt to define a way to meet the goal through a differing route, such as outsourcing parts or the entire process, doubling the capacity of a segment of production, or redefining the goal itself.

All of these efforts will help you to better know the process to a degree you never expected to achieve. And meeting the challenge of improving productivity is a great morale lift for all, as well as good business practice for the company and management.

Create equity value with every step.

You may be an architect or doctor or other professional managing your business, knowing that the end game value of your client or patient list is small and not easily transferred to any buyer without attrition. In such a case, there is little advice here unless you think outside of your day-to-day profession and create a valuable leave-behind encasing your knowledge and experience that can be replicated and scaled to a large business – even if by others.

Most businesses fall into the class of those that can be sold someday to a willing buyer. Even small community service-providers can be sold to buyers hungry to get into a business already in revenue with a steady customer base. And many businesses are created with the express purpose of growing them in size and attractiveness to be ready to sell someday to create some degree of wealth for the shareholders. Accepting venture or angel money is to create a contract between the investors and the entrepreneur that the business will someday be sold or even go public to create an exit for the investors.

This insight covers all businesses and their management when thinking of the end game, as management should during each step in the process of building the enterprise.

What creates value in a business? Is your value proposition for an eventual buyer that you have some secret sauce that allows you to compete more effectively against competition? Do you already dominate a niche, no matter how small, that a buyer will someday want for itself? Do you have intellectual property that is valuable to you but might be more so to a buyer? These questions are just a few that I'd ask during strategic planning sessions each year to fine tune the value proposition for an eventual buyer. And I'd go further. Investments into the company, whether from new money or reinvesting profits, should be directed first into areas that will increase the value of the enterprise at the end game. You do this for yourself and your shareholders, and should be thinking of this regularly.

There is always a bottleneck. Sometimes it is you.

At many board meetings, I can be counted upon to ask, "Where's the bottleneck this month?" Senior management is usually prepared with an answer, and a good discussion of resource availability and application follows. Sometimes, the bottleneck is not so visible to the CEO. In those instances, I follow with: "Do you notice people waiting at your door, telling you that they were waiting for your response or decision, even if you were unaware of this?" And occasionally, this questioning leads the CEO to realize that he or she is the bottleneck through having created a hub-and-spoke decision process, with the CEO at the center of each process. Once the bottleneck is identified, the solution often comes quickly, requiring little if any board action as management focuses resources on the bottleneck to remove the latest impediment to efficiency.

There is a great book, *"The Goal – The Process of Ongoing Improvement"* by Eliyahu Goldratt. The book was written to describe in simple terms the use of statistical analysis to remove bottlenecks in a manufacturing environment. I have used that book's lessons to teach process improvement to many types of businesses, including software development, supply chain management and retail fulfillment. I recommend that you drop everything and buy this book, read it, and if you find it as powerful as I did, purchase copies for your management team, followed by planned discussions among team members about removing bottlenecks and improving efficiency throughout the organization.

Think of the literal definition of a bottleneck in the business environment. Every resource behind the bottleneck is slowed from its most efficient pace until the resource ahead of it works its way through the constraint. In a manufacturing or production environment, that means people are stuck at their positions with completed work waiting for the process to move on. Or worse yet, more and more production is completed behind the bottleneck, only to sit as work in process, un-billable inventory of parts or services.

Behind or after the bottleneck point are people with too little to do, just like those in front of the bottleneck. But these people or machines have nothing to show for it, no way to accumulate inventory during the wait, just lost time waiting for the next process to squeeze out of the bottleneck. It is the worst form of lost opportunity within a production environment, all cost and no output.

Then there is the bottleneck itself, usually operating at maximum efficiency given the present resource size and ability to perform. If the resource is a machine and operator, would a second machine and operator remove the bottleneck and provide for a smooth flow? Add second shift at that station only? Add faster machine or faster operator? Allow fewer rejects from that point in the process? Attack the bottleneck from all angles to remove it.

The amazing thing about this process is the large amount of gain from focusing resources upon a comparatively small point of constriction - small based upon cost and time to fix. Work this question into you next management meeting and see if you are surprised by the results.

Cast your net where the big fish swim.

This is one of those "My dad used to say" homilies. You've probably heard the accompanying "It takes just as much effort to sell a small deal as a big one," over the years.

The truth of this is more nuanced. Some businesses will prosper in the shadow of larger competitors by specializing in those smaller accounts that are just not attractive to those with higher overheads and larger aspirations. But for most, the true sign of success and potential for even more is in the landing of a major account, one that validates the pricing, quality and competitive advantages of a company's offering. For this reason alone, it makes sense for most of us to aim high once we have worked the kinks out of our offering with smaller customers.

On the other hand, the worst thing you can do is land a big fish when not prepared to reel it in. It is hard to recover from any failure to perform, but doubly so when the customer is highly visible in the industry. So it is worth building the business's capabilities through stages of customer size if the goal is to serve the biggest and outdistance the competition at that level.

I am on the board of a services company that specializes in the middle of the market, knowing that very large competitors throw lots of resources at the largest accounts – resources that our company just does not have. Rather than being constantly beaten in this arena, the company has chosen to compete in an area of the market it can defend with superior service, which the larger competitors - with their higher cost structure - could not reproduce in smaller accounts without large losses. Further, scaling the enterprise and its infrastructure to go after the few very large accounts would be at the cost of development for the midrange of the market and perhaps subsequent loss of that share to others.

And I am reminded of a cousin of mine who years ago sold custom window blind product to Sears, by far his largest customer, scaling his plant to produce more and more for Sears as orders flowed. One day a sixteen wheeler full of returned product drove into his loading area. Sears, which granted a no-questions-asked return policy to its customers (even for customer errors in measuring their window blind orders) just dumped the product back on the supplier without explanation, nearly bankrupting the small company.

Even though there are many advantages to casting your net to attract the big fish, you should be well aware of the risks involved and have resources available to manage those risks.

The power of just ONE more unit.

There is such leverage in high gross profit margins once a company is past breakeven. Every dollar of gross profit falls to the bottom line, increasing net profit faster with each transaction. A ten percent increase in revenues for a company with 50% gross margin and 5% net profit before the increase would *double* net profit for the period with that ten percent increase in revenue. That's impressive sales leverage. Just to be fair, a 5% cut in costs would also double net profit.

The point is that once a company is stable at or above the breakeven point, one incremental unit generates robust increases in net profit.

In an Internet-based business, power comes not just from high gross margins, but also from an increase in the percent of conversions from "look to book," as the term is used in the hotel industry. Visit to purchase, click to close, or other terms are used in various industries to describe the measure of conversion rate from initial landing on a page displaying purchase information about a product or service. No good Internet-based business fails to measure conversion carefully and experiment with photo placement, ad words, key descriptions, product positioning – all to increase conversion.

The major focus that used to be in using the direct mail business to drive sales is now focused upon email marketing campaigns, social networking marketing, building buzz, and location-based sales using tools to recognize shoppers at the point of sale. All of these new tools are used to drive sales of the incremental unit, sales that would have been lost if not for the ability to recognize specific qualified buyers from within the general public. Cheaper marketing cost - more targeted to a ready-to-buy audience, driving incremental sales, has been made possible by the use of the Internet to seamlessly gather information and present offers at the right time to the right potential purchasers.

If you are still worrying over what tools you need to reach your potential customer, perhaps this is the time to reach out to the new class of marketing professionals who understand how to capture and utilize targeted data and present products and services to a pre-qualified audience at the right time for increasing purchase decisions.

Water flows downhill. Why fight it?

Substitute the word "money" for "water" and we have an explanation for most all of the reasons why successful products move from concept through early adopters through mass market.

Money flows to the cheapest effective solution to a problem. Fighting this fact will just extend the misery of accepting a product or marketing failure in the marketplace.

Take for example, adoption of solar panels or hybrid vehicles in the mass market. Most of us want to do well for the environment, but are willing to do so only if we do well for ourselves when measuring alternative costs. Solar panel installations break even only after over a decade of use, even with subsidies offered by electric companies or governmental organizations. And adoption of solar technology for home and business has been relatively slow as a result. As solar panel efficiency increases from 20% to 40% and more, and as electricity prices rise, the net breakeven for solar panels should decrease dramatically. Even when subsidies stop, the economic breakeven will decrease to a few years as mass acceptance becomes real. And the reason for the delays, as well as the later successes, will surely be in the money saved, not just in "doing well by doing good."

Hybrid cars become attractive investments when the extra cost can be amortized over a year or two of savings in fuel. Yes, in both cases cited, the cost of fuel is a factor as it rises over time, reducing the time to breakeven.

Whenever someone asks why a product or service has taken so long to succeed in the marketplace - when so obviously a success with early adopters - why not try using the water flowing downhill analogy. It provides a proper insight almost every time.

Turn "broadcast" into "engagement."

We all know that the world of marketing has turned upside down these past years through the power of the Internet. College professors teaching marketing must be having a real challenge keeping up with the new channels of communication, the relative values of advertising buys in this new world, and explaining how to make the most out of these cheaper and more powerful channels.

Although there is still a place for display advertising in this new world, increasingly small businesses are discovering that creating buzz and engaging their audiences through social media are more powerful and cost effective.

Marketing texts and college professors say that it takes at least seven impressions – exposures – before a person recognizes and acts upon the message. That's an expensive proposition for small companies. On the other hand, your target audience is already talking to their friends and associates about products and services they like and use. Plugging into those conversations gives you the power to multiply your message many times over, often at no cost at all.

How do you engage your customers in a conversation instead of merely broadcasting your message again and again in hope that some one remembers it? The answer comes in a number of forms, but centers around your finding the thought leaders within circles of influence, attracting the "influencers" that people follow. To do this, your message must resonate in a way that it appears unique.

If you cannot incorporate social content into your product, surround your product with social content. Create groups in Facebook, followers on Twitter, a comments section on your blog or website, and more. Identify a number of influencers, and then offer to let them use your product or service at low or no cost if they will join your informal advisory group on the 'net. Ask for endorsements when appropriate.

Above all, make every outreach an attempt to engage your customers, listening to their responses and responding one-to-one wherever possible. Make each customer feel important and valued. In this new world of engagement marketing, the customer has a voice much earlier and much louder than ever before.

Measuring your power in the Internet marketplace.

There are a number of key performance indicators that help new generation company management see more clearly their progress and corporate health. The old measures, including return on investment, percentage of profit against revenue or employee count, and more, obviously are still relevant. But businesses that expose their story to tens of millions of potential customers through the Internet need additional tools. Some of these are also applicable to non-Internet businesses.

Here are some of these measures, and how to calculate them. You will recognize the value of these for any business, even if they have not been in common use in the past.

- CHURN (% customer cancelling each month)

    - This is calculated by dividing the number of cancellations by the total number of customers before cancellations and multiplying by 100.

- CMRR (Contracted Monthly recurring Revenue)

    - A simple statistic which can be derived from a good general ledger using GAAP accounting procedures. Revenues are recorded as earned, not paid, especially when paid in advance. This number is increasingly used by appraisers and buyers in valuing a business, with some multiple of this number being one measure of the value of the enterprise.

- LPC (Lifetime Profit per Customer)

    - This is the total expected revenue for a customer (usually calculated with a five year life no matter what the type of business) less the cost of acquisition (see below) less the recurring direct costs of serving the customer or of product estimated to be sent to the customer over the lifetime relationship.

- CACR (Customer Acquisition Cost Ratio)

    - This is a measure of capital efficiency, focusing upon the cost of acquisition of the customer (including direct sales, commission payable, direct marketing and other direct costs) divided by the expected gross revenues over the customer's estimated lifetime of purchases. The lower the ratio, the more successful the customer acquisition campaign.

- CPA (Cost per Acquisition)

- This is simply the sum of the month's direct costs for sales and marketing divided by the number of new customers acquired, yielding a dollar cost per average new customer. The lower, the better.

- MBE   (Months to breakeven)

  - A better measure of capital efficiency. Total new customers this month times the average expected revenue - divided by total direct sales and marketing cost together with the cost of product or service for those customers for the month. The result will yield the number of months the average account takes to be profitable for the company.   The lower the number, the more efficient the marketing and sales campaign, and the more efficient the use of financial capital in customer acquisition.

Surely some of these measures would, if used by your organization, shed additional light on the efficiency of the operation and over time the trends related to efficiency.

Create and nurture your collective intelligence.

At the MIT Center of Collective Intelligence, professors and graduate students are wrestling with an important opportunity – and gaining ground. With new collaborative tools available for use in the cloud, people are no longer isolated in their creative endeavors. Some label this "crowdsourcing," a term used to describe one form of this new empowerment.

How do you use the new tools for collaboration to enable people and computers to be connected so that collectively they act more intelligently than any individual? MIT has come a long way in identifying tools and techniques.

You can do the same. First, realize that no individual in your organization, including yourself, is as effective alone as with collaborative help from peers. Then find ways to build concepts, plans, documents, and actions through the collective collaboration of your key group. Explore and implement one of the many collaborative environments available through cloud computing, products from Microsoft, Google, IBM, and others.

Test the system. Create a document with your basic plan or idea for action. Post the document using one of these common tools and invite members of your group to add to or comment upon this beginning effort. Respond and build upon the result. You will note that within a short time, you will have created a plan or document usually far better than if you had worked alone. And the added benefit is that the group will feel ownership in the result, a powerful step toward a successful outcome.

Create a Powerful Dashboard.

From sports car to aircraft to super tanker, successful operation depends upon the pilot's understanding and urgent timely use of a dashboard. Real time information is critical to real time decision-making, and increasingly in the modern business world, decisions are made by management without extended meetings or discussion with others.

And with the rise of modern technology-driven businesses, the same is true of management in the business world. A good dashboard of relevant real time information is now available for most any business, often created by computer software from data derived from monitoring real time tasks within the business.

You should consider creating such a dashboard, or reviewing the one you use if already driving with one at hand. I've developed four criteria for use in creating and evaluating your dashboard. When constructing yours, you should consider the following:

1. <u>Controllable outcomes:</u> There is no use for information for which there is no ability to control changes as a result of analysis. Ensure that you include only information for which you have a way to alter future outcomes in a positive direction. An example would be a real time display of the value of the dollar against the yen. If your business has no trade with Japan that could be affected by arbitrage, early shipments or other tactics that take advantage of the moving value of these currencies, that statistic is irrelevant to the dashboard – even if interesting to you.

2. <u>Earliest warning metrics:</u> What good is information if you can't act upon it in a timely manner? Find metrics that will be "leading indicators" of trouble to come. Think of labor efficiency (future product or service delivery impairment) or warehouse inventory (sales slowdown, supply chain management problems) as examples.

3. <u>Items in the critical path (bottlenecks):</u> This is one of my focus issues for my workshops, it is so important. One of your chief duties is to remove bottlenecks in the delivery process for your product or service, enabling all resources before and after the bottleneck to achieve maximum efficiency. If a critical path machine is slow or down, your own email box overflowing with questions from subordinates needing answers, or any other measure of critical path impairment in need of fixing, you should know about it at the earliest possible moment. Add a measure of each that you identify with to your dashboard.

4. <u>Items impacting cash (now or later):</u> Cash is the oil of your business. Slowing of production, deliveries, raw materials, receivables collections, billing for work completed – all are going to influence cash flow soon and should be tracked when out of expected range.

Simple indicators that affect multiple areas above include increasing backlog, call center delay time denigration, increases in finished goods inventory amounts, unbalanced work in process inventory buildups, and reduced efficiencies in billed time for consultants or experts.

How about projecting cash on your dashboard: cash on hand plus expected accounts receivable collections less necessary accounts payable payments less payroll. You will find many more candidates for your personal dashboard. Try to limit yours to five or fewer critical measures that can be updated no less often than daily if not in real time.

You will be steps ahead of most of your competitors and in a much better place to succeed if you create and maintain an effective dashboard.

Growth requires a different kind of capital.

Growing companies usually require more working capital during their periods of rapid growth. In past insights we have calculated the amount of additional capital needed for a business as it grows, and the additional capital required is often surprisingly large. In this insight, we need to speak of the sources of working capital and the implications to the future financial health of the choices made when selecting one financial resource.

Venture or angel-financed companies with plenty of working capital sometimes are immune to this need for some time into their growth, but at some point it will become clear that the cheapest form of finance is not equity in a growing enterprise. If the equity value of a company is growing at the same rate as the company, say 40% per year, almost any form of debt financing may be preferable as a way of preventing further dilution from issuing additional equity.

The problem is that few small, growing companies seem to be attractive to most banks for traditional unsecured or asset-backed loans. The exception is for those venture-backed companies with a significant cash balance remaining in the bank, which ironically make the most attractive customers for banks to offer loans. The banks want to maintain their venture relationships and of course, want to use the existing company cash in their bank as collateral for – you guessed it – their loans to the company. The term of art is "compensating balances," and certainly using existing cash to leverage new loans makes the company more liquid, but at a price, as the compensating balances cannot be touched and are essentially frozen for the duration of the bank loan.

There are asset-based lenders of every size willing to take more risk and finance the growth of young companies without requiring compensating balances. Using the company's receivables and inventories as collateral, such lenders often also ask for a uniform commercial code (UCC) filing, perfecting their first interest in all of the remaining assets of the company - including intellectual property, the latter often being by far the most valuable asset the company has to protect.

Loan covenants are always required that clearly state how much net equity, the minimum current ratio, and other minimum financial requirements must be maintained to be compliant, and state the penalties for non-compliance - which are always severe, often threatening to call or cancel the loan in its entirety.

One of the important items in a calculation of amounts available to be borrowed is the amount of qualifying collateral, defined usually as the amount of net accounts receivable less than 60 days old, after deducting government billing - and all receivables from companies with some balances over 60 days. To this net number, the lender will then apply a percentage, from 50% to 80% as the amount available for borrowing under the agreement.

It is important to calculate the true cost of such money. It is typical to charge an interest rate that is higher than a normal bank loan for asset-based loans. Also tacked on is a "float period," typically two to five days, amounting to additional interest as if the money paid back is still outstanding for that time as compensation for the time to clear checks paid into the lender either by your customers directly (lock box method) or by you. A five day float increases the actual interest rate by up to an additional 2% over the stated rate. Then there is the loan audit fee, often more than $4,000 a year, to pay for the lender's auditor to make sure the collateral and company are compliant with the covenants of the loan. Lenders sometime add a charge for loan oversight, called a consulting fee, and very often make warrants (a promise to later sell the lender stock at a fixed price) a part of the deal. When calculating the true cost of a working capital loan, after adding all of these elements and estimating the value of the warrants in dilution to the shareholders, you may be shocked at the number when expressed as an annual percentage rate.

And yet, such a loan does rise and fall with need. And it is often cheaper than the cost in dilution of issuing additional stock to obtain working capital. These decisions require knowledge by management, help from accountants and or attorneys, and an understanding at the start of such a relationship that borrowing from asset-based lenders is like entering a marriage where the other partner has all the power to ensure success in the event that anything goes wrong with the original plans.

About the author...

Dave Berkus has a proven track record in operations, venture investing and corporate board service, both public and private. As an entrepreneur, he has formed, managed and sold successful businesses in the entertainment and software arenas. As a private equity investor, he has obtained healthy returns from liquidity events in over a dozen investments in early-stage ventures. As a corporate mentor and director, he was named *"Director of the Year"* for his directorship efforts with over 40 companies in the past decade.

Dave was the founder of **Computerized Lodging Systems Inc.,** *(CLS),* which he guided as founder and CEO for over a decade that included two consecutive years on the *Inc.500* list of America's fastest growing companies, expansion to six foreign subsidiaries and twenty-nine foreign distributors, while capturing 16% of the world market for his enterprise products. Known as a hospitality industry visionary with many "firsts" to his credit and for his accomplishments in advancing technology in the hospitality industry, in 1998 he was inducted into the **Hospitality (HFTP) "International Hall of Fame,"** one of only thirty so honored worldwide over the years.

He has made over 100 investments in early stage ventures, for which he has an IRR of 97%, which includes capital contributions to his two funds (**Berkus Technology Ventures, LLC** and **Kodiak Ventures, L.P.**, for which he is the managing partner). He is also Chairman Emeritus of the Tech Coast Angels, one of the largest angel networks in the United States.

In recognition for adding significant shareholder value for emerging technology companies over the past decade, he was named **"Director of the Year-Early Stage Businesses"** by the *Forum for Corporate Directors* of Orange County, California and **"Technology Leader of the Year"** by the Los Angeles County Board of Supervisors. Dave currently sits on ten corporate boards and four non-profit boards.

Dave is also a senior partner in the twenty year old consulting firm of *Hospitality Automation Consultants, LTD (HACL)*, and lends his considerable visionary and strategic talents to worldwide hospitality chains and groups. He is the partner responsible for business process reorganization, strategic planning, software development and wide-area network infrastructure, and enterprise management systems.

A graduate of Occidental College, Dave currently serves as a Trustee of the College. Aside from this book, he is author of fourteen other books, twelve in the **BERKONOMICS** series, *"Extending the Runway"* originally published by Aspatore Press (and now by the BERKUS Press), and co-author of *"Better than Money!"* All are books for emerging growth technology company executives. Dave serves as Board Member of the San Gabriel Valley Council of **Boy Scouts of America**, former Board Member of the **Forum for Corporate Directors,** and is Chairman of the Advisory Board of the technology arm of the **ABL Organization**, a networking organization of CEOs in high tech businesses.

He is often engaged as keynote speaker for events worldwide, speaking on trends in technology and of legal and practical issues of governance for emerging company corporate boards. He tells stories of entrepreneurs who have wildly succeeded or failed, deriving lessons from each for his audience. His TEDx talk, *"Smile at success; Laugh at failure,"* is available on YouTube as are other of segments of his keynotes. His televised *"Berkus Report"* segment of *Eye on Business*, can be found on Time Warner cable and other cable channels nationwide.

To contact Mr. Berkus for speaking engagements or workshops, email dberkus@berkus.com , or phone (626)355-5375. Dave's books are available for purchase from the above website, or the same source from which this book was purchased.

Subscribe to the free weekly email or blog, www.Berkonomics.com, containing much of the information from Dave's books with lots of comments from readers with their own stories to tell.

Follow Dave on Twitter (@daveberkus) and Facebook (Dave.Berkus).

Other books by Dave Berkus available directly from *www.berkus.com* or from your favorite bookseller or online store:

EXTENDING THE RUNWAY
Aspatore Press / Thompson West Publications

The five tools board members and executives can use to help their companies succeed.   How boards and CEOs should relate to each other for growing the enterprise. Fifty-eight critical questions boards and management should consider in order to assure their mutual alignment.

BASIC BERKONOMICS
Hard cover, soft cover and eBook editions

Volume one of this series. Over one hundred critical insights for entrepreneurs, CEOs and board members covering the life of the company from ignition through liquidity event.   Written with basic explanations for terms and methods, as well as insights into planning and measurement for success with small business startups.

BERKONOMICS
Hard cover, soft cover and eBook editions

Volume two of this series. One hundred and one critical insights for entrepreneurs, CEOs and board members covering the life of the company from ignition through liquidity event.   Dave tells over fifty stories to illustrate his insights, culled from his experience as entrepreneur and service on over forty corporate and ten non-profit boards.

BERKONOMICS WORKBOOK

Companion to BERKONOMICS, this very personal journal contains 101 exercises for the CEO or manager that make each of the insights contained in BERKONOMICS come to life in the form of provocative and actionable questions to be answered right on the pages of the workbook. Once completed, this workbook becomes the manager's personal blueprint for business growth.

ADVANCED BERKONOMICS

Hard cover, soft cover and eBook editions

Volume two of this series. One hundred and one critical insights for entrepreneurs, CEOs and board members covering the life of the company from ignition through liquidity event.   More advanced insights into planning and measurement for success with small business startups.

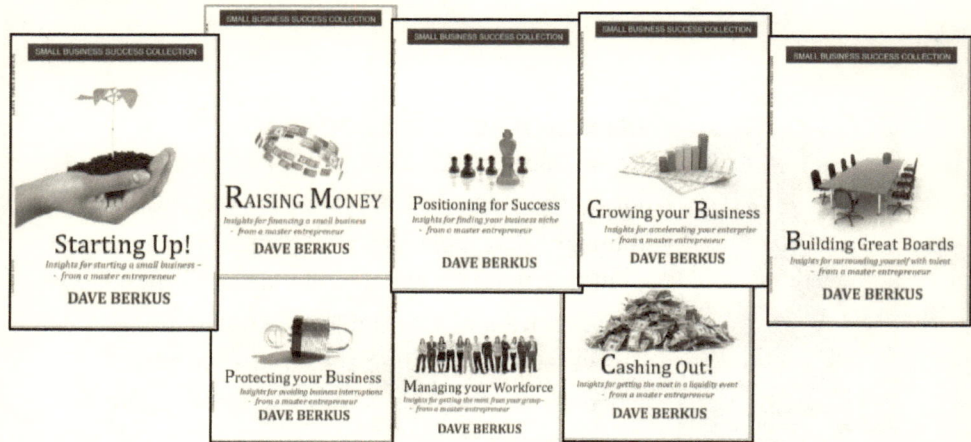

SMALL BUSINESS SUCCESS SERIES
A Series of eight short and inexpensive books or eBooks

Take all the great material in the BERKONOMICS series and slice it by subject, and you'll have these eight inexpensive, short books about issues that you and your management team needs to focus upon today. Ideal for giving to your entire management group for group discussions and business planning sessions.

BOOKS and eBOOKS IN THIS SERIES:

1. *Starting up!*
2. *Raising Money*
3. *Positioning for Success*
4. *Managing your Workforce*
5. *Protecting your Business*
6. *Growing your Business*
7. *Building Great Boards*
8. *Cashing Out!*